How To Take Your Online

ABRSM Music Theory Exam

Grades 1, 2 & 3

(Exam Techniques for Everyone)

by

Sharon Bill

How To Take Your ABRSM Online Music Theory Exam

Grades 1, 2 & 3

(Exam Techniques for Everyone)

by Sharon Bill

www.SharonBill.com

© 2017 Sharon Bill

© Revised 2021 Sharon Bill

Illustrations by Billy

www.BillyArt.co.uk

© Billy 2017 & 2021

In this Music Theory Exam Technique Guide I do not address the technical demands of the on-line exam. Everyone has a different set-up in terms of internet provider and personal computer. Be sure to test the systems and download the relevant software as stipulated by ABRSM. This is the student's/responsible adult's responsibility, not the responsibility of the tutor or ABRSM.

This book is not a guarantee of exam success but is a guide to support your study. It builds upon the principle that you have worked through the relevant ABRSM Discovering Music Theory Workbooks and have revised the material necessary for the ABRSM Theory examinations.

Contents

INTRODUCTION

This exam preparation guide presumes that you have worked through the ABRSM Discovering Music Theory workbooks. These are available from the ABRSM online store, any online music dealer or your local music shop.

For help in progressing through these ask your music tutor. You can also download my **FREE** PDF Information Sheets from;

www.SharonBill.com

and you can watch my step-by-step tutorials to guide you through the workbook on Youtube at;

www.YouTube.com/SharonBill

ABRSM Grade 1 ABRSM Discovering Music Theory workbook provides the first foundation in music theory.

ABRSM Grade 2 ABRSM Discovering Music Theory workbook presumes a working knowledge of all that was covered in Grade 1 **plus** the new material presented in Grade 2.

ABRSM Grade 3 ABRSM Discovering Music Theory workbook presumes a working knowledge of all that was covered in Grades 1 and 2 *plus* the new material presented in Grade 3.

Once you've completed the workbooks…

YOU'RE READY TO THINK ABOUT TAKING THE EXAM

There are lots of past exam papers available to buy at a very reasonable price. You can order previous exam papers for many year's exams from the ABRSM online shop, online music stores or your local music retailer. There are also sample practice papers freely available direct from ABRSM's website. Work through some past exam practice papers as revision and practise for exam timing. Use the tips from this exam guide and treat the past papers as mock exams. Work as if you were actually sitting the exam.

- Always write in pencil. Use a sharp pencil and have a ruler and an eraser handy. Although the actual exam is completed on a computer, the practice exam papers are written. The principle of answering the questions is exactly the same. Always use pencil for both your scrap paper and your exam paper. Keep your working out and exam paper neat. Use an eraser for any corrections - untidy working leads to confusion and mistakes.

- Find a quiet desk or table and make sure you have at least an hour and a half of uninterrupted time.

- If the first paper you attempt takes longer than the allocated exam time don't worry, you will get quicker with practise. Attempt a few more papers over time and you will soon find your stride.

• Follow ALL of the instructions as described in this guide as if you were actually sitting the exam. Don't skip any steps thinking, "It doesn't matter for a practise paper."

No Peeping! Complete each past paper without assistance. It is better to make some mistakes and to then learn from them. If you peep and look up some answers you are only learning passively and will soon forget again.

PERFECT PREPARATION PREVENTS

POOR PERFORMANCE

Success is always dependant upon hard

work and effort

Calculate how much time you spend on watching TV or browsing through social media. If you spend too much of your time on these things it will be reflected in your results.

The only place that Success comes before Work is in the dictionary!

There are lots of past exam papers available to buy at a very reasonable price. You can order previous exam papers for many years' exams from the ABRSM online shop, online music stores or your local music retailer. Use as many as it takes until you feel confident of your results. Answer booklets are available but only purchase these (if you choose to purchase them at all) after you have completed the papers so you aren't tempted to peep.

You can also make good use of the previous style exam papers which pre-date the new exam format. These are excellent for revision and also give you extra practice on writing neat notation. Some of the questions the older papers no longer appear on the new exam syllabus, you can just skip these questions - the majority of the content is still applicable and provides valuable extra revision opportunities.

Although Model Answer papers are available and can be helpful, if you don't understand *how* your answer was incorrect refer back to the relevant section in your work-book to revise the principle of the question or refer to the PDF information sheets I have provided. You can also watch the appropriate YouTube tutorial I have provided for the work book and selected past papers. Alternatively, talk through the paper with your music tutor. Find out *why* the answer you wrote was incorrect and *learn* from your mistake.

In the exam there are a total of 75 marks available.

To pass you need to score 50/75

To pass with Merit you need to score 60/75

To pass with Distinction you need to score 65/75

It is not unusual for my pupils to pass with Distinction and many have scored 100%

EQUIPMENT REQUIRED

Pencil cases

and mobile phones are

NOT ALLOWED

in the exam room

Neither are you permitted to reach into pockets.

This is to make sure that no cheating takes place.

You can either put all the items you need for the

exam into a small, clear, plastic bag or you could

keep them all together tied in an elastic band.

In addition your computer (and webcam) you will also need:

- A piece of A4 paper

- At least two sharp pencils. (Don't bother taking a pencil sharpener as you don't want to be troubled with sharpening pencils during the exam.)

- An eraser.

- A ruler.

- A watch. (As mobile phones are not allowed in the exam room it is a good idea to have a watch or clock to keep track of time.)

- You might choose to take a bottle of water into the exam with you. If you do have a bottle of water only take sips to refresh yourself as you don't want to waste time drinking and you can't nip to the loo!

SITTING THE ABRSM EXAM

Before the exam begins you need to carefully follow the directions given by ABRSM, including scanning the room, desk space and scrap paper, to show that you have nothing in the room by which any means of cheating may occur. You then need to personalise your screen options for aspects such as font size, background screen colour and other such presentation details. Once these steps are completed you may then begin your exam and the timer now starts.

DO NOT ANSWER

ANY QUESTIONS YET

Follow my suggested exam procedure to prevent time wasting and to maximise the marks you will score.

If you simply go ahead and answer the first questions you see you risk losing valuable marks.

WORKING THROUGH

YOUR EXAM

 The time allocated for the ABRSM Grades 1, 2 and 3 is an hour and a half. You have plenty of time so there is no need to rush.

Take a deep breath and enjoy the experience. As my dear Nan used to say, "It's all in life's rich pattern."

Follow the system outlined in this booklet for working through your exam. This method is tried and tested and always gives the best possible marks. I repeat that it is not unusual for my students to gain Distinction and even score 100%.

DO NOT

Begin to Attempt To Answer Any

Questions Yet

Use your scrap paper to jot down certain facts that you will constantly be referring to throughout the exam. Do this in your mock exam practise at home. After all of your mock exam practise you should be quite used to quickly noting down the information you need.

For my degree exam I spent weeks practising what I referred to as my "Quick Draw." I needed to be able to refer to a number of musical quotations and I needed to get them onto paper quickly so that I could feel free to address whatever questions might arise, knowing that my reference material was already 'out of my head.' I called it a "Quick Draw" because I felt like a Wild West gun slinger: When the glove was dropped (or the timer started) I would reach for my pencil, like a Colt 45, and quickly scribble out what I needed before nerves took over and made me forget. I was quite chuffed when, after many practise attempts, I got 3 sides of manuscript covered in musical quotations within 15 minutes.

 In doing this you only have to think about these important details once. They are now handy for you to refer to each time you need to think about these things as they recur throughout the exam paper. This saves valuable time in the exam as you won't need to keep trying to recall them to memory every time a question raises the point, you can just refer to your notes. In this way you also prevent unnecessary stress and confusion.

All of this will only take

about five minutes

Scrap Paper for Grade One

In Grade 1 your scrap paper might look like this. However, you may quickly jot down anything you will find particularly helpful.

Scrap Paper for Grade Two

In Grade 2 your scrap paper might look like this. However, you may quickly jot down anything you will find particularly helpful.

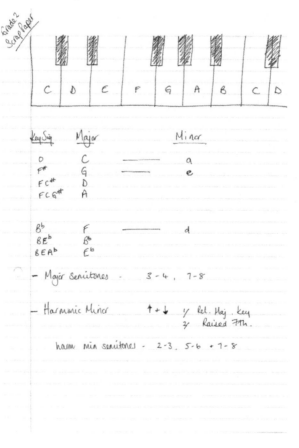

Scrap Paper for Grade Three

In Grade 3 your scrap paper might look like this. However, you may quickly jot down anything you will find particularly helpful.

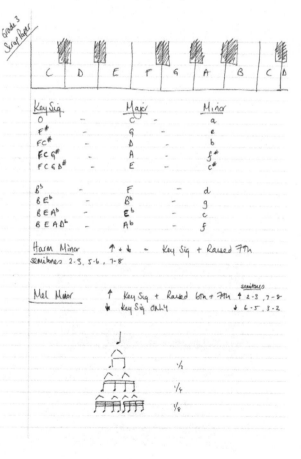

BEGINNING THE EXAM

YOU MAY NOW Read Through The Exam

Questions

BUT

YOU MUST NOT YET ATTEMPT TO

ANSWER ANY QUESTION

Read through ALL of the questions but do not answer any question.

You can easily toggle between the screens.

There are two reasons for reading through the all of the questions before attempting to answer any question

- Our brain is far more capable than we credit. If you "input" the information that the whole paper requires your brain can be processing that information. Once you begin to answer the first question your brain can already be "thinking" about all of the other questions instead of reacting to new information each time you come to a new section.

- There may be information in a later question which could help you in a section at an earlier part of the exam paper. If you are struggling with an answer a clue which may help you could be triggered from a later section. If you haven't read your paper all through you might miss out on some helpful hints.

This process shouldn't taker longer than ten minutes. You are now only fifteen minutes into the exam and have over an hour remaining. You have already done most of the hard thinking.

You have plenty of time!

RE-WORKING THE EXAM

You Must Now Work Through Your Exam

A *Second* Time

You May Now Begin To Attempt The

Questions In Your Exam

Don't necessarily begin with question 1. Answer any question that you can easily answer. However, if you find a question particularly difficult place a marker/flag next to this question and then skip on to the next section. It is important that you only work on the questions that you are confident about and skip any questions you do not easily know.

There are two reasons which make it beneficial to work through an exam in this way

- There is no point wasting time stressing over a question that you are unsure of when you could be completing questions which you are confident about and would be gaining you maximum marks. For example, if you spend a disproportionate amount of time on question one but, as you do not readily know the answer and you may not score good marks, you have misused the exam time. It is better to use the exam time in answering questions which will gain you the best marks. Spend the time wisely and answer the questions you are sure of first. Later you can use what time you have available to make the most of these trickier questions.

- If you become stressed at the start of an exam it is bound to impair your judgement and prevent you from achieving your best. For example, if you have spent a long time worrying about the first question and know that you haven't much time left you will be concentrating on the clock more than thinking about your exam questions. Also, even though you would have been confident in your answers for the later questions you will now be stressed which will cloud your memory and cause you to be less effective for the rest of the paper.

When working with multiple choice answers ALWAYS work out the solution to the question yourself first. Don't look at the answer options until you have done so.If you look that the multiple choice answers first this makes you inclined to guess and actually confuses you more. In turn, this could lead to confusion, stress and ultimately will waste valuable exam time.

Always have a pencil, eraser and some scrap paper to hand to help you work out the answer for yourself. You are allowed to have a blank piece of paper with you in the digital exam. You must show this to the camera before the exam begins, as an unmarked sheet, to prove that no cheating is occurring. Once the exam has commenced you can write down anything from memory that you may find helpful. (See later chapter for how to make best use of your scrap paper sheet.)

If You Don't Know The Answer, Skip It... *(for now)*

RE-WORKING THE EXAM...

AGAIN

You Must Now Work Through Your Exam

For A *Third* Time

Return to the start of your exam and complete any answers that you have missed, removing the marker/flag once each question is completed. It is highly likely that something will have jogged your memory and you now know how to go about answering the questions that you previously skipped.

If you still don't know the answer...

GUESS!

 Never, ever leave an empty space where an answer is required. An empty space is guaranteed to score zero marks whereas a guess may score a few unexpected points. It is probable that your guess will be more informed than you imagine but even if your guess is hilariously wild it will still merely score no points and nothing has been lost in the attempt. You might even give the exam marker a smile to brighten their day as they plough through a pile of marking.

Experience has shown me that, if you have worked through the appropriate workbooks, worked through past exam practice papers and have revised thoroughly, you will have more than sufficient time.

You should still have time to spare!

CHECKING THROUGH

THE EXAM

You Must Now Work Through Your Exam

For A *Fourth* Time

Although you have completed all of the questions in the exam you must now quickly read through all questions and check your answers. Check you haven't missed a question.

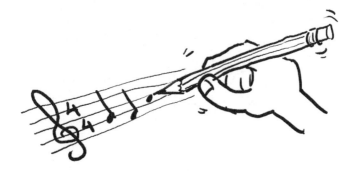

YOU HAVE NOW COMPLETED YOUR

EXAM

CONGRATULATIONS!

If you work through your exam paper

ONLY ONCE

it is an absolute certainty that you will not have given sufficient attention to the exam questions and you

WILL BE THROWING AWAY
VALUABLE MARKS!

EXAM ORDER RECAP

In order to score maximum points you should follow this system:

- Before you begin your exam jot down relevant information, on a piece of scrap paper, to refer to throughout the exam.

- Read through every question in the exam, but answer NOTHING until you have read every question.

- Work through your exam answering only those questions which you easily know. Any question that you are unsure of mark for later attention and skip to the next.

- Go back to the beginning of the exam. Answer any questions that you have missed. If you still don't know the answer, GUESS. Never leave a space where an answer should be.

- Read your exam through for a final time. Check it for mistakes and make sure that is is neat and easy to read.

This method will help to give you the best results

I say again, it is not unusual for my students to gain Distinction and even score 100%

There is no reason why this shouldn't be you!

WELL DONE!

At this point it is usual to wish you "Good Luck" but an exam is never down to luck. Success is always dependant upon correct preparation. So I'll wish you "All The Best" in your revision and exam journey.

Remember

Perfect

Preparation

Prevents

Poor

Performance

If you have studied your music theory, revised adequately, practised your exam technique with ABRSM Past Exam Practice Papers, and have worked through your exam in a tried and tested procedure you don't need luck.

If you have followed the procedure outlined in this guide, if you have prepared thoroughly and have sat the exam in the manner I've suggested:

You have worked hard

Enjoy the results of your efforts!

RESOURCES

ABRSM Discovering Music Theory

for Grades 1, 2 and 3.

Available from ABRSM http://shop.abrsm.org

or most online or local music stores

ABRSM Music Theory Past Exam Practice

Papers

Available from ABRSM http://shop.abrsm.org

or most online or local music stores

Model Answers to ABRSM Music Theory Past

Exam Practice Papers

Available from ABRSM http://shop.abrsm.org

or most online or local music stores

FREE PDF Information sheets

to accompany each section in the

ABRSM Theory in Practise workbook at

www.SharonBill.com

FREE YouTube tutorials taking you step-by-step

through each section in the ABRSM Theory in

Practise workbook and selected ABRSM Music

Theory Past Papers at

www.YouTube.com/SharonBill

Also Available by Sharon Bill
from Amazon in Paperback & eBook

A summer fête in rural Cheshire, organised by the Women's Institute of Mossleigh, holds the promise of an idyllic day out in the best British tradition. Everyone is enjoying the festivities until a beloved neighbour is found dead among the bins and refuse of the village hall which saddens the holiday mood. However, it is only when Beth Williams and her twin brother Detective Chief Inspector Benedict James join forces that it becomes evident that all isn't as innocent as it at first seemed.

Beth is a piano tutor and a member of the local WI. As such she has her finger on the pulse of the undercurrents of the village and is ideally placed to find all of the seemingly inconsequential domestic details which could give her brother the insight he needs. Together, if they each pool their own particular fields of expertise, they're bound to get to the bottom of the business. Sordid crime might prevail amid the pastries and preserves for a time but, in the end, the culprit will get their just desserts.

Also Available by Sharon Bill
from Amazon in Paperback & eBook

Mere hours after a Constable watercolour sketch is featured in a presentation at a meeting of Mossleigh Women's Institute the original is stolen from the Whitworth Art Gallery. It seems that the cultured veneer of the art world shields a much seedier underworld where theft is just the icing on the cake. Beth and her twin brother, DCI Benedict James, join forces to get to the bottom of the affair. Although DCI James must pursue the official lines of enquiry Beth finds that a more abstract approach draws the threads of the mystery together.

Beth is a piano tutor and member of her local WI and is aptly placed to tap into seemingly insignificant details to get right to the heart of the affair. When all hope fades and the Old Masters look to be forever tainted by sordid crime Beth, with the help of her unassuming friends, restores the balance of justice and the intrinsic beauty of artistic endeavour.

Also Available by Sharon Bill
from Amazon in Paperback & eBook

They say that truth is stranger than fiction. Nearly 30 years of teaching at the piano keyboard has taught me that this is an undeniable fact. My dear Gran said that the world would be a boring place if we were all the same and teaching piano and flute in various cupboard like practice rooms, week in and week out over the years, reassures me that there is no threat of humanity becoming dull. If I present a wry viewpoint of various past pupils it is only fair to say that I also take an equally droll approach to myself.

Letters From the Broom Cupboard was the given title to an actual correspondence from my piano teacher during her own periods of incarceration in the privation of various school practice rooms which served to fill the looming periods of pupil absenteeism. This literary offering continues the legacy and I now write to you, dear reader, in my own hour of need.

Also Available by Sharon Bill
from Amazon in Paperback & eBook

Check out **Sharon's YouTube channel** for a free accompanying series of music theory tutorials. You are guided, step by step, through the ABRSM Music Theory workbooks. Each video tutorial leads you through each exercise and free to download PDF information sheets give you everything you need to know.

There are lessons explaining all aspects of music theory and practical music topics which are simply explained so as to be easily understandable in 4k.

For everything you need to help you with your ABRSM Music theory visit....
www.YouTube.com/SharonBill

For more information about Sharon Bill's

Writing, Blog and Music Tuition &

Free PDF Downloads

www.SharonBill.com

Facebook @SharonBillPage

Twitter @SharonEBill

Instagram @sharonbill_ig

YouTube Channel showing tuition videos in 4k

www.YouTube.com/SharonBill

All video & social media page links are also

available at www.SharonBill.com

Printed in Great Britain
by Amazon